1 **Blue tit**

Found in woodland, parks and gardens. Watch it hopping quickly through trees. It often drinks cream from milk bottles.

2 **Great tit**

The largest tit, with yellow underparts and a black stripe down its breast. It has white cheeks and a black head. It is common in woods, parks and gardens.

3 **Long-tailed tit**

A little, fluffy, pink and black bird with a tail that is longer than its body. Where did you find yours?

4 **Coal tit**

Look for the white patch on the back of its black head. Often found in fir trees as it eats the seeds in ripe cones which it gets out with its beak.

5 **Goldfinch**
It is easy to recognize this bird. It has a scarlet face and black and white head. Watch for the yellow bars on its wings.

6 **Greenfinch**
A bright yellow-green bird which you can recognize by the yellow flashes on its wings and tail. Look also for its short, pointed beak, for eating seeds.

7 **Chaffinch**
The male has a chestnut-coloured breast and its head is blue-grey. Look for two white bars on the wings of both the male and the duller female. Did you see a male and a female?

5

15

20

6

8 **Bullfinch**

Look for its red front, black head and white bar on each wing. The female is paler than the male. They feed on berries, buds and seeds.

10

7

8

9 **Robin**

The robin is well known for its red breast and face. Look for one in woodland, parks and gardens. Some can be quite tame and will come close to you if you are quiet and still.

10 **Wren**

Although it is a very small bird, the wren sings very loudly. It is common in woods and gardens where it likes hedges and thick undergrowth. Look for its short upright tail.

9

10

10

20

11

5

10

12

11 **House sparrow**

A very common bird. It is brown with a grey crown, black bib and a white bar on its wings. It nests under roofs, in holes and nest boxes, or builds nests in bushes and trees. Do you think it looks cheeky?

12 **Linnet**

In spring, the male has a red crown and breast, but this colour fades by autumn. A linnet is a little smaller than a sparrow. Found in open areas with bushes or low trees. Where did you find yours?

10

20

13 **Dunnock**

Also known as a hedge-sparrow, this is a common bird in woods and gardens. It has a grey breast and speckled flanks. You can tell it from a sparrow by its thinner beak.

14 **Chiffchaff**

A greenish-brown bird usually with black legs. It is very common in woodland, where it can hide in trees among the twigs and leaves. Listen for its song of ‘chiff-chaff chiff-chaff’.

15

10

20

16

15 Yellowhammer
This is common on farmland and other open country with bushes. It is bright yellow with a brown back. Its song is often thought of as 'little-piece-of-bread-and-no-cheese'. Did you hear its song?

16 Stonechat
Look for one on heaths, moors and also on cliffs by the sea. The male has a black head and chestnut breast with some white marks. The female is paler. Did you see a male and a female?

5

17

15

18

5

19

17 **Song thrush**

This is a common garden bird, but also lives in open country where there are trees. Look for its speckled breast. You may see it breaking snails on a stone.

10

18 **Field fare**
Watch out for one especially on farmland. Look for its blue-grey head and rump and chestnut back.

19 **Blackbird**
It is easy to recognize the male. He is glossy black with a bright yellow beak and eye-ring. The female is a bit like a thrush but has less obvious speckles on her breast. It is common in gardens, parks and woods.

20 **Starling**
This is often seen in towns as well as in the country. It is a very noisy bird. Look for its short tail and the purple shine on its feathers in summer. In winter it is spotted. When did you see yours?

21 **Swift**
A swift has longer thinner wings than a swallow or house martin (both illustrated). Also, it is brown not blue, and does not have white underparts. Look for a flock of swifts near towns and villages. They build their nests in hollow trees, chimneys and other protected places. They can fly very fast.

22 **Swallow**
A swallow has a red face and a long forked tail. In autumn, swallows gather to fly south together. You may see some perched on telegraph wires. In summer, they are very common on farmland.

23 **House martin**
Watch for this bird in summer. It is common on farmland and in towns, and builds a mud nest under the eaves of buildings. Notice its dark blue back and white underparts and rump. It has a slightly forked tail which you can see when it flies.

24 **Skylark**
Look and listen for a skylark in open country as it does not perch in trees. It is a brown bird with a small crest, and sings a musical song high up in the sky.

25 **Pied wagtail**
This is a small black and white bird with a long tail which wags up and down. The female has a dark grey back, but the male has a solid-black back.

20

21

15

22

10

23

25

24

25

15

26

20

27

10

28

10

29

20

26 **Jay**

Look for a jay in woodland and large gardens. Pinkish, with dark wings and tail, it is not a good flyer and is very noisy. Where did you find yours?

27 **Wood pigeon**
The largest and most common pigeon. It has a pink breast and blue-grey body, and a white mark on its neck. Seen in towns and cities as well as woods.

28 **Magpie**
It is very easy to recognize this bird. It is black and white with a long tail. You may see a pair together and sometimes more. How many did you see?

29 **Collared dove**
This is a sandy-coloured bird. Look for its black half-collar, and white band on the underneath of its tail.

30 **Cuckoo**
The cuckoo comes to Britain in the summer. Look for a grey bird in woods and on moorland and listen for the male's famous 'cooc-ooo'. In what month did you first hear one?

25

31 **Osprey**

This is a fascinating bird to watch. Look out for one near lakes and rivers especially in Scotland. However, you may see one on its way to or from Africa, where it spends the winter.

It has dark brown upperparts and white underparts which are lightly marked on the wings and tail. Look for its white head with a dark stripe through the eye. Its main food is fish. It hovers low over the water, and when it sees a fish, it drops feet first to grasp it with

50

its powerful talons. If you see one flying, look at its wings. They are long and slender and held so that they slope up and then down like a flattened letter M.

Score 50 if you see an osprey.

15

32

20

33

15

34

30

32 **Rook**

A large glossy-black bird with heavily-feathered legs and a white patch on its face. You will see flocks of rooks. Look for their nests in the tops of trees.

33 **Carrion crow**

Another black bird. This one has no white on its face or extra feathers on its legs. Look for pairs of crows in open country.

34 **Jackdaw**

This bird is very common in open woods, towns and around farms. It is black. Look for the grey patch on the back of its neck and on the sides of its face.

35 **Raven**

A very large black bird that likes undisturbed areas especially highlands. Look for its large head and beak.

30

36 **Hen harrier**
Often seen hunting, when it glides low over the ground. Found in open country and over marshes and swamps. Where did you see your hen harrier?

37 **Tawny owl**
The most common owl in Britain, it has a rounded head with black eyes. Listen at night for its hooting in woods and parks.

38 **Kestrel**
You may find a kestrel in a town, as well as around trees and cliffs. It has long pointed wings and a long tail, and hovers above the ground looking for prey. Look for its large head and eyes and powerful beak.

39 **Buzzard**
Found in wooded areas, but also in open areas in winter. Look for the broad rounded wings and tail when it is flying. Buzzards are usually brown, but some are very pale and some are very dark.

30

37

25

38

39

30

30

40

41

25

42

25

20

40 **Green woodpecker**
This woodpecker is often seen on the ground, feeding on ants. It has green wings and a bright yellow rump. Also look for the small red patch on its head.

41 **Great spotted woodpecker**
The most common woodpecker. It is a black and white bird with a red patch under its tail. In spring, listen for the sound of it drumming on a tree.

42 **Treecreeper**
Unlike the nuthatch, this bird only creeps up trees not down. Watch out for one in woodland, flying from the top of one tree trunk to the bottom of another.

43 **Nuthatch**
Has a blue-grey back and chestnut-coloured underparts. Uses its long beak to pick insects from tree bark. Watch for it walking up and down tree trunks, searching for food.

25

44

44 **Red grouse**

Common on upland moors and heaths. It likes heather to nest in and for cover, and also for food. Look for one on farmland in winter. A heavy-looking bird, rather like a chicken.

45 **Pheasant**

A pheasant is easy to recognize. Both male and female have long pointed tails. The male is very

15

45

46

20

colourful with a red eye patch on a green head. It is common in open woods and farmland. Did you see a male or a female?

46 **Partridge**

This has a rusty-coloured tail, orange-brown throat and face, and a chestnut patch on its belly. You may find pairs or family groups on any open land. Look for them running along the ground.

47

47 **Greylag goose**
The most common goose. It is a heavy-looking bird with an orange beak and pink legs. Look for it on farmland, grassland, wetland and estuaries.

48 **Pochard**
A very easy duck to recognize. It has a chestnut head, grey body and a black chest and tail. The female is paler than the male. Look on lakes, ponds and streams for one.

49 **Mallard**
The mallard is the most common duck. The male has a green head, white collar and brown breast. In summer, he moults and then looks just like the female, but you will know him by his yellow beak.

20

48

49

5

50 **Avocet**

A black and white bird with very long legs and a long upturned beak. It sweeps this from side to side through water to catch its food, such as shrimps. Watch out for one on estuaries and salt marshes.

51 **Curlew**

In spring and summer you may find one on wet moorland. In winter, look by the sea in wetlands and estuaries. It has long legs and a long down-curved beak which it uses to catch worms in the mud.

52 **Lapwing**

Watch out for one in meadows, marshes, moors and fields. In winter it can be found near water. Look for its long thin crest. It is often called a peewit. Did you hear its loud 'pee-wit' call?

53 **Shelduck**
Watch out on shores and estuaries for one. It swings its beak from side to side through mud to catch its food of tiny snails. The male has a knob on its beak.

54 **Gannet**
A large white seabird which is easy to recognize by its pale-orange head and the black ends of its wings. Watch for it diving into the sea to catch fish.

55 **Common tern**
Look for a bird flying gracefully over the surface of the sea. It may rise suddenly, then dive into the sea to catch a fish. Notice its forked tail.

56 **Herring gull**
Common by the sea. Look for its yellow beak and pink legs. Herring gulls remain paired for life.

15

53